It's all about…

EPIC EXPLORERS

HIGH LIFE HIGHLAND	
3800 16 0040729 4	
Askews & Holts	Mar-2017
	£4.99

KINGFISHER

First published 2017 by Kingfisher
An imprint of Macmillan Children's Books
20 New Wharf Road, London N1 9RR
Associated companies throughout the world
www.panmacmillan.com

Series editor: Sarah Snashall
Series design: Anthony Hannant (LittleRedAnt)
Adapted from an original text by Chris Oxlade

ISBN 978-0-7534-3933-3

9 8 7 6 5 4 3 2 1

1TR/0916/WKT/UG/128MA

A CIP catalogue record for this book is available from the British Library.

Printed in China

Picture credits
The Publisher would like to thank the following for permission to reproduce their material.
Top = t; Bottom = b; Centre = c; Left = l; Right = r
Front cover Alamy/Royal Geographical Society; Pages 2–3, 30–31 iStock/kaetana; 4 iStock/
Daniel Prudek; 5t Alamy/Inferfoto; 5b Alamy/Granger Historical Archive; 6 iStock/Flemming
Mahler; 7c Alamy/B Christopher; 7b iStock; 8–9 JrPol; 9 iStock/LMG Photos; 10 Shutterstock/
Rudra Narayan Mitra; 11c Getty/DEA Picture Library; 11b, 12–13, 14–15, 16–17 Kingfisher
Artbank; 13 Alamy/World History Archive; 17t Alamy/Classic Image; 18–19 iStock/Kenneth
Canning; 19 Kingfisher Artbank; 20 Getty/Superstock; 21 ESA; 22 Shutterstock/Przemyslaw
Skibinski; 23 Alamy/Granger Historical Picture Archive; 24, 25 Alamy/Classic Image;
25t Alamy/Pictorial Press; 26–27 NASA; 28 iStock/Predrag Vuckovic; 29t NASA; 29 Alamy/
Jeff Rotman.
Cards Front tl Alamy/Franck Fotos; tr Alamy/North Wind Picture Archives; Back tl iStock/
Georgios Kollidas; bl Alamy/Everett Collection; br NASA.

You will find c. before some dates. This stands for *circa*, which means 'about'.

Life dates: Throughout this book, you will see dates in brackets after an explorer's
name. These tell you when they lived. For example, Marco Polo (1254–1324) means
that Marco Polo was born in 1254 and died in 1324.

Front cover: English explorer Ranulph Fiennes pulls a sledge on his 1990 expedition
to the North Pole.

CONTENTS

Great explorers

Since the beginning of history explorers have travelled across deserts and through rainforests, over mountains, oceans and frozen lands to explore unknown lands.

Explorers were often away from home for many years. Sometimes they didn't have accurate maps and faced terrible weather, disease or hunger. Many died on their expeditions.

view of Mount Everest

In 1325, the Moroccan traveller and scholar Ibn Battutah set off from Morocco and headed for Persia.

Sir Edmund Hillary and Tenzing Norgay on Mount Everest

SPOTLIGHT: Ascent of Mt Everest

Leaders:	Edmund Hillary and Tenzing Norgay
When:	29 May 1953
Total length:	two days from base camp
Final height:	8848 m

In ancient times

Some of the first explorers were Polynesian people who settled on islands in the Pacific Ocean about 3500 years ago. They sailed across hundreds of kilometres of open seas, from island to island, in large sailing canoes.

FACT...

The travels of Chinese discoverer Chang Ch'ien opened up the Silk Road – the great trading route between China and the Mediterranean.

Later, people from Ancient Egypt sailed up the River Nile, searching for precious goods such as gold, spices and perfumes. The Ancient Greeks and Romans and the Phoenicians all explored the lands around the Mediterranean Sea.

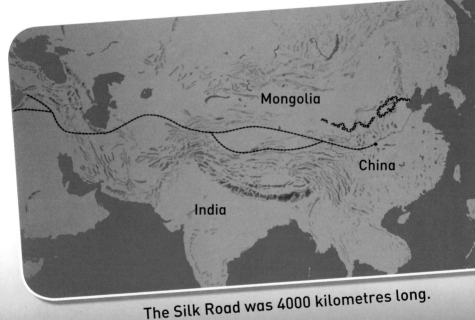

The Silk Road was 4000 kilometres long.

Camels were used to transport silk and other goods across the desert.

Viking voyages

The Vikings lived in Scandinavia more than 1000 years ago. They were expert ship-builders and sailors. They sailed to Britain, France, Spain, Russia and Iceland.

In 982CE a Viking called Erik the Red sailed from Iceland with his family. He landed in the south of Greenland where he built a Viking settlement.

The remains of a Viking settlement in Greenland.

Viking ships were very sturdy, with space on deck for goods and livestock.

FACT...

In about 1000ᴄᴇ, Erik's son, Leif Eriksson, sailed to Newfoundland – he was probably the first European to land in North America.

Marco Polo in China

Marco Polo was born in Venice, in modern-day Italy. In 1271, when he was just 17 years old, he set off to China with his father and his uncle. In 1275, four years after the start of his journey, he arrived at the court of the Mongol emperor, Kublai Khan.

Marco Polo crossed the mountains of Afghanistan and travelled along the Silk Road.

Marco Polo stayed in China for 17 years, travelling around the country and reporting back to Kublai Khan. He saw many new things such as kites, fireworks and paper money. These were Chinese inventions that he'd never seen before.

Stories of Marco Polo's adventures were written down in the *Book of the Wonders of the World.*

FACT...

Marco Polo worked as a spy for Kublai Khan.

Marco Polo bows before the powerful emperor, Kublai Khan.

Columbus and America

In 1492, an Italian called Columbus set out to search for new lands for Spain. After 35 days at sea, his ship's crew saw an island. Columbus was trying to reach Asia, but he had actually found one of the Caribbean islands that are now called the Bahamas. He had discovered America for the Europeans.

Columbus says farewell to Isabella, Queen of Spain, before setting sail.

Altogether there were about 90 men on Columbus' three small ships. Columbus had a small cabin, but the crew slept on deck, wherever they could find a space. They ate biscuits, dried meat and any fish they could catch.

Christopher Columbus and his men crossed the Atlantic Ocean in a ship called the *Santa Maria*.

First around the world

In 1519, Portuguese adventurer Ferdinand Magellan sailed from Spain to the southern tip of South America and found a sea passage through to the Pacific Ocean.

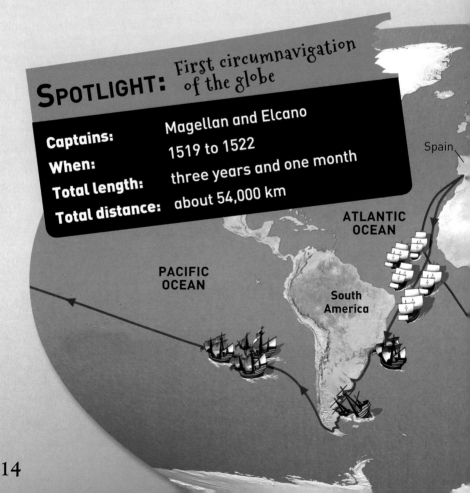

SPOTLIGHT: First circumnavigation of the globe

Captains:	Magellan and Elcano
When:	1519 to 1522
Total length:	three years and one month
Total distance:	about 54,000 km

Spain

ATLANTIC OCEAN

PACIFIC OCEAN

South America

For five months Magellan and his sailors crossed the Pacific Ocean. Many of them died from hunger or disease. They finally arrived in the Philippines, where Magellan was killed in a fight with local people. Two ships continued the journey, and one finally returned to Spain in 1522.

Cook in the Pacific

James Cook was a captain in the British navy. In 1768, Cook set off to explore the Pacific Ocean. During three journeys, he sailed south to the Antarctic Circle, sailed around New Zealand and charted the east coast of Australia and the west coast of Alaska.

cutaway view of Cook's ship, *HMS Endeavour*

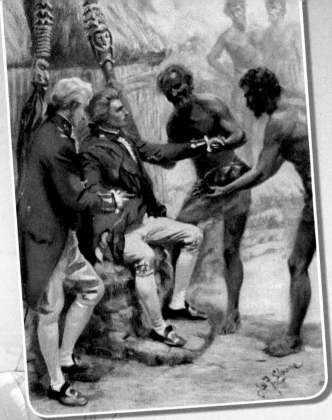

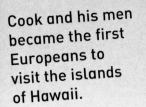
Cook and his men became the first Europeans to visit the islands of Hawaii.

FACT...

Captain Cook was murdered in Hawaii during a row about a stolen boat. He was 50 years old.

17

Lewis and Clark

In 1804, Meriwether Lewis and William Clark travelled across the northwest half of the North American continent. They planned to survey the area, and to find a route to the west coast.

FACT...

Sacagawea, a Native American girl, guided the explorers through the Rocky Mountains.

The two explorers set out from the American town of St Louis in May 1804, with 43 soldiers. They eventually reached the Pacific Ocean in the autumn of 1805.

Lewis and Clark and their expedition team paddled up the Missouri river in canoes.

The Northwest Passage

For hundreds of years explorers searched for a sea route around the north of America. It seemed impossible to navigate through this maze of islands and frozen seas.

In 1845, English explorer John Franklin set off with two ships and 128 men. Tragically, the ships became stuck in the ice and everyone died.

Franklin and his men abandoned their ships and tried to walk to safety.

Norwegian explorer Roald Amundsen finally completed the journey through the Northwest Passage in 1906. He sailed in a boat with just six men.

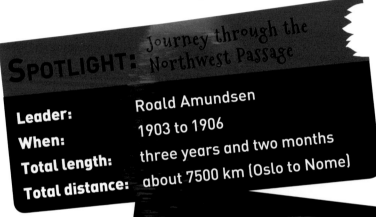

SPOTLIGHT: Journey through the Northwest Passage

Leader: Roald Amundsen
When: 1903 to 1906
Total length: three years and two months
Total distance: about 7500 km (Oslo to Nome)

This satellite picture shows the route of the Northwest Passage.

FACT...

The effects of global warming mean that the Northwest Passage is now often ice-free and navigable during the summer months.

African adventures

Many explorers from Europe went to Africa in the 1800s, including David Livingstone and Mary Kingsley. Over many years, Livingstone crossed the Kalahari Desert, travelled down the great Zambezi river and discovered the towering Victoria Falls. He died while searching for the source of the River Nile in 1873.

David Livingstone was the first European to see the magnificent Victoria Falls.

FACT...

In 1895 Mary Kingsley fell into an animal trap.
Her thick skirt saved her from being injured
by the sharp spikes at the bottom of the pit!

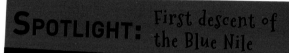

SPOTLIGHT: First descent of the Blue Nile

Who:	Lead explorer Pasquale Scaturro
Start:	Ethiopia, 25 December 2003
End:	Egypt, 28 April 2004
Distance:	5230 km

Mary Kingsley explored the Ogowe river in
Gabon, in about 1895.

Race to the South Pole

In 1911, Norwegian Roald Amundsen and Briton Robert Scott raced to reach the South Pole. Both teams struggled for weeks, battling over mountains and glaciers. Amundsen finally reached the South Pole on 14 December 1911.

Scott arrived at the South Pole 34 days later to find the remains of Amundsen's camp. Scott and all his men died on the return journey back to their base camp.

Amundsen's team travelled swiftly on skis and with dog sledges.

Leader:	Roald Amundsen
When:	14 December 1911
Total length:	99 days (base camp return)
Total distance:	3440 km (base camp return)

Scott and his team ran out of food and were caught in terrible blizzards.

Armstrong on the Moon

In 1969, Neil Armstrong became the first person to stand on the surface of another world – the Moon. It took two days to travel to the Moon, then Armstrong and 'Buzz' Aldrin descended to the Moon's surface in their lunar module.

Around 500 million people watched astronaut Neil Armstrong on TV as he walked on the surface of the Moon.

Astronauts plan to visit Mars – but they might not be able to come home again.

SPOTLIGHT: Moon landing

Commander:	Neil Armstrong
When:	21 July 1969
Total length:	eight days
Total distance:	1,533,791 km

FACT...

In 1985, Neil Armstrong walked to the North Pole with mountaineer Sir Edmund Hillary.

Undiscovered places

There are still many undiscovered places in the world: mountains in Colombia, deserts in Namibia, parts of the Amazon rainforest, strange caves in Mexico and much of the ocean floor – and almost all of the rest of space.

These divers are exploring underwater caverns in the Yucatán Peninsula in Mexico.

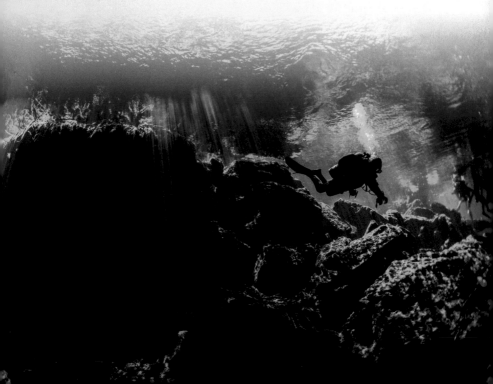

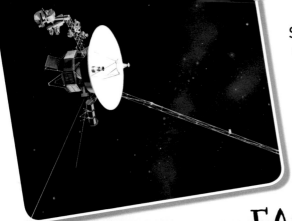

Space probe *Voyager 1* was the first object made by humans to leave the Solar System.

FACT...

Film director James Cameron reached the bottom of the Challenger Deep, nearly 11 kilometres under the Pacific Ocean.

The *DeepSee* submersible records data and images of creatures in the Pacific Ocean.

GLOSSARY

CE Short for 'Common Era' (any date after 1CE). It is also sometimes known as AD (anno domini, or after Christ).

Challenger Deep A part of the Mariana Trench that is the deepest known part of the ocean.

circumnavigation The act of travelling around something, for example the world.

expedition A journey that is taken for a special purpose, such as to explore a place.

global warming The slow warming-up of the Earth in recent years.

Kublai Khan A very powerful emperor of China, who lived in the 13th century CE.

livestock Farm animals.

lunar module The section of spacecraft that took astronauts between the command module and the Moon's surface.

Native American An original inhabitant of the North American continent.

navigate To plan a travel route through an area that is difficult.

Phoenician People who lived in the ancient country of Phoenicia, on the eastern coast of the Mediterranean Sea.

Polynesian A person from an area of the Pacific Ocean that includes Hawaii, Samoa and the Cook Islands.

sea passage A narrow sea route between islands or other land masses.

settlement A place, previously uninhabited, where people have settled and built a group of houses.

Silk Road An ancient trading route between China and eastern Europe, named after the silk that was transported along the route.

space probe A robot spacecraft sent to another planet or moon, to take photographs and collect scientific information.

submersible A small underwater vehicle that can withstand the ocean's pressure.

survey To examine an area in order to make a map.

INDEX

Collect all the titles in this series!

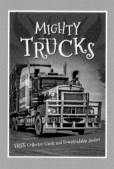

BEASTLY BUGS

FREE Collector Cards and Downloadable Audio!

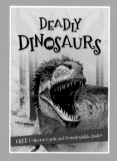

DEADLY DINOSAURS

FREE Collector Cards and Downloadable Audio!

EPIC EXPLORERS

FREE Collector Cards and Downloadable Audio!

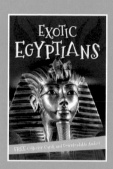

EXOTIC EGYPTIANS

FREE Collector Cards and Downloadable Audio!

FANTASTIC FLIERS

FREE Collector Cards and Downloadable Audio!

FAST CARS

FREE Collector Cards and Downloadable Audio!

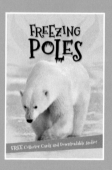

FREEZING POLES

FREE Collector Cards and Downloadable Audio!

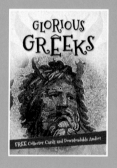

GLORIOUS GREEKS

FREE Collector Cards and Downloadable Audio!

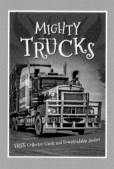

MIGHTY TRUCKS

FREE Collector Cards and Downloadable Audio!

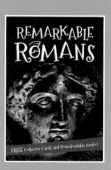

REMARKABLE ROMANS

FREE Collector Cards and Downloadable Audio!

RIOTOUS RAINFOREST

FREE Collector Cards and Downloadable Audio!

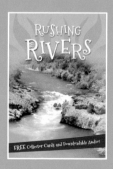

RUSHING RIVERS

FREE Collector Cards and Downloadable Audio!